Forest Bright
Forest Night

By Jennifer Ward

Illustrated by Jamichael Henterly

Dawn Publications

For Taylor, who loves books. – JW

For fire lookouts, ever watching
over the bright forest,
night forest. – JH

A Sharing Nature With Children Book

Library of Congress Cataloging-in-Publication Data

Ward, Jennifer, 1963-
  Forest bright, forest night / by Jennifer Ward ; illustrated by Jamichael Henterly.-- 1st ed.
    p. cm. -- (A sharing nature with children book)
  ISBN 1-58469-066-6 -- ISBN 1-58469-067-4 (pbk.)
 1. Animals--Juvenile literature. 2. Nocturnal animals--Juvenile literature. I. Henterly, Jamichael, ill. II.
Title. III. Series.
  QL49.W29 2005
  591.5'18--dc22

2004019024

Dawn Publications
12402 Bitney Springs Road
Nevada City, CA 95959
530-274-7775
nature@dawnpub.com

Printed in China

10 9 8 7 6 5 4 3 2 1
First Edition

Design and computer production by Patty Arnold, Menagerie Design and Publishing

Sun light, forest bright,
After sleeping through the night,

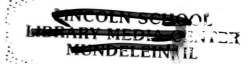

Leap and flash ... deer splash

Climb and stumble ... bear cubs tumble

Whittle and rap ... woodpeckers tap

Slither and slip ... snakes whip

Jabber and talk ... blue jays squawk

Store and stash ... squirrels dash

Chatter and chase ... chipmunks race

Strut and wobble ... turkeys gobble

Buzz and dip ... bees sip

Roost and nest ... quail rest

Sun sinks,
Moon winks,
Hello, forest night.

Many forest animals are awake during the day.
They sleep at night, as we do.
Many other forest animals are awake at night.
When do they sleep? They sleep during the day!

By day...

While a deer leaps through the forest, an owl sleeps in a tree.

While bears climb and tumble, porcupines sleep in a tree or burrow.

While woodpeckers rap and tap, opossums sleep in a tree hollow.

While snakes slither, foxes sleep in an underground den.

While blue jays jabber, skunks sleep in a den under rocks or logs.

While squirrels dash, salamanders sleep underground
or under plants.

While chipmunks chase, mice sleep in
an underground burrow.

While turkeys gobble, beavers sleep
in a lodge made of sticks.

While bees buzz, crickets sleep.

While quail roost, frogs sleep
under plants or in
a burrow.

FLIP THE BOOK
FOR FOREST NIGHT

Many forest animals are awake during the night.
They sleep during the day.
Many other forest animals are awake during the day.
They sleep at night!

At night...

While an owl is awake and hooting, a deer sleeps in a thicket.

While porcupines plod around the forest, bears sleep in a den.

While opossums climb, woodpeckers sleep in a tree hollow.

While foxes prowl, snakes sleep under a rock, log or in a burrow.

While skunks scurry, blue jays sleep in a tree nest.

While salamanders hide, squirrels sleep in a nest of
leaves up in a tree.

While mice munch, chipmunks sleep
in an underground burrow.

While beavers swim,
turkeys sleep in a tree.

While crickets call,
bees sleep in a hive.

While frogs
hop, quail
sleep in a
nest on
the ground.

FLIP THE BOOK
FOR FOREST DAY

Moon goes down,
Sun grows round,
Hello, forest day.

Flip and flop ... frogs hop

Jump and crawl ... crickets call

Paddle and swim ... beavers trim

Nibble and crunch ... mice munch

Slither and slide ... salamanders hide

Scurry and scramble . . . skunks amble

Yip and yowl ... foxes prowl

Climb and sneak ... opossums peek

Parade and plod ... porcupines trod

Hoot and perch . . . owl eyes search

Moon bright, forest night,
After sleeping through the light,

As a child, Jennifer spent lots of time exploring in nature and often wrote stories about what she saw. Sometimes she wrote them just for herself. Sometimes she gave them to her parents. Also as an adult, Jennifer immersed herself in nature. She became a teacher but eventually decided to write full time for children. She is now the author of several popular children's books. Jennifer Ward has a fun website, www.jenniferwardbooks.com.

Jamichael Henterly never intended to be a book illustrator. He was an Army paratrooper, an infantry medic, a firefighter and a Forest Service fire lookout. He wanted to be a scientist, but he loved to draw, and somehow "blundered into" illustrating as a career. Jamichael does lots of research when he illustrates. He says that "to draw like an artist helps you to see like a scientist, and to see like a scientist helps you to draw like an artist. I strive to capture in my pictures the same beauty and wonder that captivates and excites me as an observer of nature." He lives along a wild river near Deming, Washington.

A FEW OTHER NATURE AWARENESS BOOKS FROM DAWN PUBLICATIONS

Under One Rock: Bugs, Slugs and other Ughs by Anthony Fredericks, illustrated by Jennifer DiRubbio. No child will be able to resist looking under a rock after reading this rhythmic, engaging story.

Seashells by the Seashore by Marianne Berkes, illustrated by Robert Noreika. Children comb the beach, counting and identifying shells, and appreciating the creatures that lived in them.

Earth Day, Birthday by Pattie Schnetzler, illustrated by Chad Wallace. To the tune of "The Twelve Days of Christmas," here is a sing-along, read-along book that honors the animals, the environment, and a universal holiday all in one fresh approach.

The John Denver & Kids Series - John Denver's most child-friendly and nature-aware lyrics are adapted and illustrated as picture books by Christopher Canyon. Currently in release: *Sunshine On My Shoulders* and *Ancient Rhymes: A Dolphin Lullaby.*

The Okomi Series with Jane Goodall - Jane Goodall's actual observations of chimpanzee families are touchingly presented for very young children through the character of Okomi, a young chimp, in a series of eight small volumes. By Helen & Clive Dorman, illustrated by Tony Hutchings, in cooperation with the Jane Goodall Institute.

Dawn Publications is dedicated to inspiring in children a deeper understanding and appreciation for all life on Earth.
To view our full list of titles or to order, please visit our web site at www.dawnpub.com, or call 800-545-7475.

Forest Night
Forest Bright